¿HABLAS ESPAÑOL?

The *South Beach* method for Conversational Spanish

By: Erasmus-Cromwell Smith

This course is radically different from any others as you will be taking steps backwards to revisit a bit of English Grammar in order to refresh certain rules and practices of our language.

As you will see, there are plenty of things we say simply because we are used to but on many of them, we don't know whether they are right or even why we speak that way.

The premise is simple, we go back and revisit our language to refresh or learn certain concepts to translate English properly into Spanish. Our own language construction has to be grammatically right (properly built), otherwise what will come out in Spanish will be equally wrong!

Conversational Spanish

➢ This course will enable you to speak Spanish within hours.

➢ This course debunks the idea that Spanish is a very hard language to learn.

➢ Actually, in most cases, both languages are spoken in the same way (literally like a mirror image).

➢ The Foundation of this method is the Infinitive Verbs.

➢ You will learn to speak through 4 templates (all of them using Infinitive Verbs).

➢ The method also teaches you how to pronounce/spell properly in Spanish.

➢ It also allows/enables you to study/learn most Spanish Verbs only in Infinitive Form (almost without conjugations) effectively cutting thousands of hours and thousands of verb conjugations from the learning process.

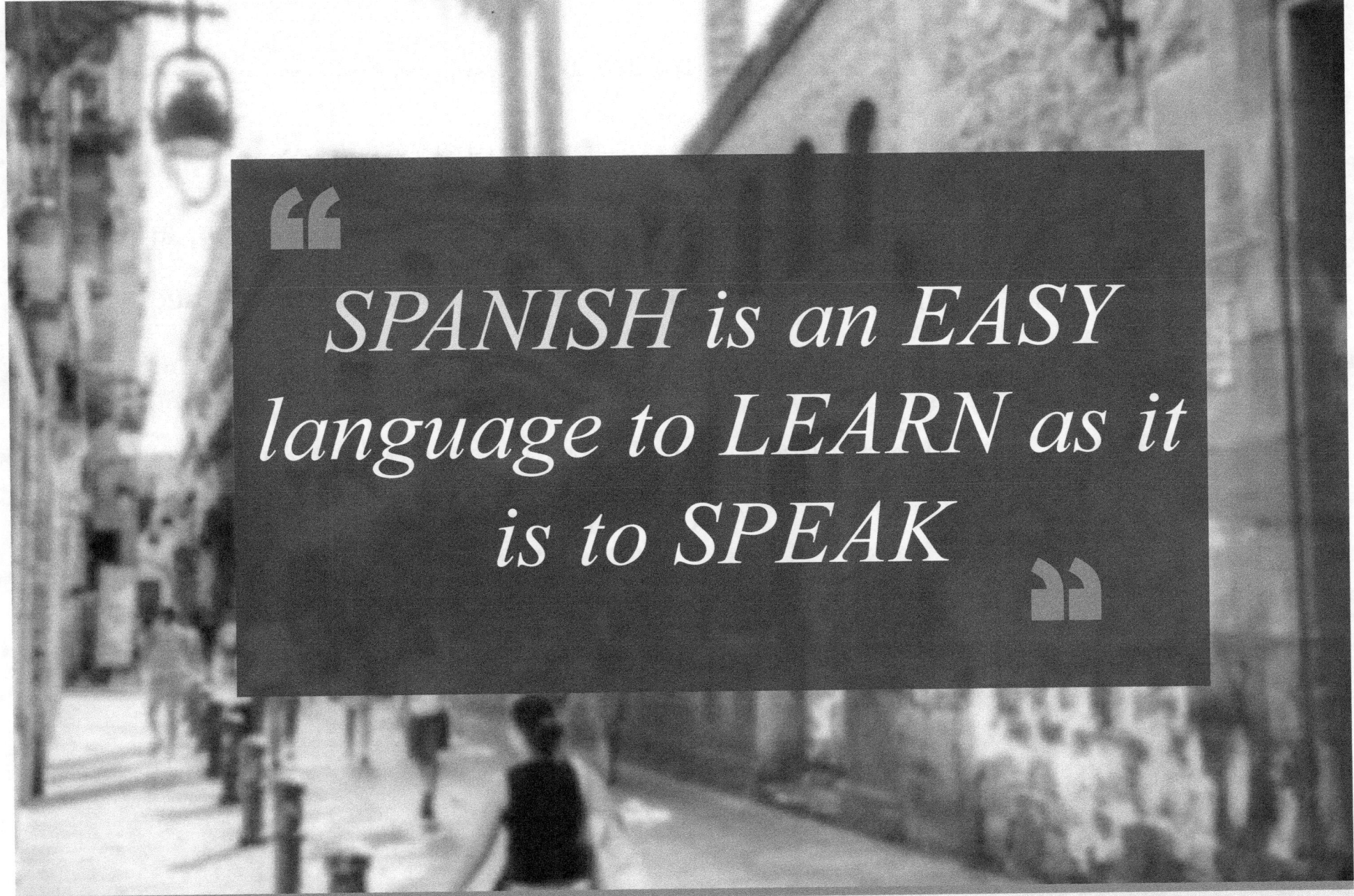

> " **SPANISH** *is an* **EASY** *language to* **LEARN** *as it is to* **SPEAK** "

Let Us Begin...

For the most part :

➢ Spanish is spoken the same way English is!

➢ Most of the grammar rules (even their names) are the same.

➢ Phrases are structured the same way.

➢ Many, many words are very similar if not the same.

Spanish difficulty debunked:

Spanish vowels have only one sound: **AH-EH-E-OH-UH**

English has two or more sounds per vowel!

So, let's debunk the idea that Spanish is so difficult!

Learning Step 1

Everything Begins With

The 5 Vowels

Next you will learn how to pronounce them easily!

Lesson 1: Part 1

The Basics First: "The Vowels"

Spanish Vowel	Spanish Pronunciation		Easy: Pronunciation is in parenthesis ( )		
A (AH) Read Aloud	Ah Again	Ah Again	Ah Again	Ah Again	Ah
E (EH)	EH	EH	EH	EH	EH
I (E)	E	E	E	E	E
O (OH)	OH	OH	OH	OH	OH
U (UH)	UH	UH	UH	UH	UH

Now let's practice them one after the other: **AH-EH-E-OH-UH**

Now do it faster: **AH-EH-E-OH-UH** now even faster: **AH-EH-E-OH-UH**

Keep on practicing : **AH-EH-E-OH-UH** ' until you memorize it .

AH-EH-E-OH-UH Repeat and memorize the sound.

AH-EH-E-OH-UH Try to do it faster & faster.

Learning Step 2

Next is to learn

The Alphabet

Pronunciation in Spanish is in (parenthesis)!

Pronunciation and phonetics of the Spanish Alphabet

A (ah)	B (beh)	C (zeh)	D (deh)	E (eh)	F (efe)
G (heh)	H (ache)	I (e)	J (hota)	K (ka)	L (ele)
M (eme)	N (ene)	O (oh)	P (pe)	Q (koo)	R (ere)
S (ese)	T (teh)	U (oo)	V (ve)	W (doble-ve)	
X (ekeys)	Y (e-gree-eh-gah)		Z (zeh-tah)		

Learning Step 2

It is also very useful to learn

The Numbers

Uno One	Dos Two	Tres Three	Cuatro Four	Cinco Five	Seis Six	Siete Seven	Ocho Eight	Nueve Nine
Diez Ten	Veinte Twenty	Treinta Thirty	Cuarenta Forty	Cincuenta Fifty	Sesenta Sixty	Setenta Seventy	Ochenta Eighty	Noventa Ninety

Cien One hundred	Doscientos Two hundred	Trescientos Three hundred	Cuatrocientos Four hundred
Quinientos Five hundred	Seiscientos Six hundred	Setecientos Seven hundred	Ochocientos Eight hundred
Novecientos Nine hundred	Mil One thousand	Diez mil Ten thousand	Cien mil One hundred thousand
Un millón One million	Cien millones One hundred million	Mil millones/Un millardo One billion	Un trillón One trillion

Learning Step 3

Having learned the alphabet and the vowels, the next step is to learn:

The Nouns

I - You	
	Easy , just read it ! ()
Read it aloud	Read it aloud
I - Yo (Yoh)	You – Usted-(oosted)
Read it aloud	Read it aloud
I - Yo (Yoh)	You – Usted-(oosted)
Read it aloud	Read it aloud
I - Yo (Yoh)	You – Usted-(oosted)
Read it aloud	Read it aloud
I - Yo (Yoh)	You – Usted-(oosted)
Read it aloud	Read it aloud
I - Yo (Yoh)	You – Usted-(oosted)
Read it aloud	Read it aloud
I - Yo (Yoh)	You – Usted-(oosted)
Read it aloud	Read it aloud
I - Yo (Yoh)	You – Usted-(oosted)
Read it aloud	Read it aloud
I - Yo (Yoh)	You – Usted-(oosted)

Remember in Spanish I is **Yo**, *You is* **Usted**

He - She	Easy , just read it ! ()
Read it aloud He – El (ehl)	Read it aloud She – Ella (eyah)
Read it aloud He – El (ehl)	Read it aloud She – Ella (eyah)
Read it aloud He – El (ehl)	Read it aloud She – Ella (eyah)
Read it aloud He – El (ehl)	Read it aloud She – Ella (eyah)
Read it aloud He – El (ehl)	Read it aloud She – Ella (eyah)
Read it aloud He – El (ehl)	Read it aloud She – Ella (eyah)
Read it aloud He – El (ehl)	Read it aloud She – Ella (eyah)
Read it aloud He – El (ehl)	Read it aloud She – Ella (eyah)

*Remember in Spanish <u>He</u> is <u>**El**</u>, <u>She</u> is <u>**Elle**</u>*

We - You	Easy , just read it ! ()
Read it aloud	Read it aloud
We – Nosotros (Noh-soh-trohs)	You – Ustedes
Read it aloud	Read it aloud
We – Nosotros (Nohsohtrohs)	You – Ustedes
Read it aloud	Read it aloud
We – Nosotros (Nohsohtrohs)	You – Ustedes
Read it aloud	Read it aloud
We – Nosotros (Nohsohtrohs)	You – Ustedes
Read it aloud	Read it aloud
We – Nosotros (Nohsohtrohs)	You – Ustedes
Read it aloud	Read it aloud
We – Nosotros (Nohsohtrohs)	You – Ustedes
Read it aloud	Read it aloud
We – Nosotros (Nohsohtrohs)	You – Ustedes
Read it aloud	Read it aloud
We - Nosotros (Nohsohtrohs)	You – Ustedes

Remember in Spanish <u>*We*</u> *is* **<u>Nosotros</u>**, <u>*You*</u> *is* **<u>Ustedes</u>**

Lesson 2: Part 4

They - It	Easy , just read it ! ()
Read it aloud They - Ellos (eyohs)	Read it aloud It - Eso/Esto
Read it aloud They - Ellos (eyohs)	Read it aloud It - Eso/Esto
Read it aloud They - Ellos (eyohs)	Read it aloud It - Eso/Esto
Read it aloud They - Ellos (eyohs)	Read it aloud It - Eso/Esto
Read it aloud They - Ellos (eyohs)	Read it aloud It - Eso/Esto
Read it aloud They - Ellos (eyohs)	Read it aloud It - Eso/Esto
Read it aloud They - Ellos (eyohs)	Read it aloud It - Eso/Esto
Read it aloud They - Ellos (eyohs)	Read it aloud It - Eso/Esto

*Remember in Spanish <u>They</u> is **<u>Ellos</u>**, <u>It</u> is **<u>Eso/ Esto</u>**

Lesson 2

SUMMARY	The Nouns		Easy, just read it! ()
Let's continue to practice!	I - Yo	(Yoh)	Repeat it 5 times!
	You - Usted	(Oosted)	Repeat it 5 times!
	He - El	(Ehl)	Repeat 5 more times
	She - Ella	(Eyah)	This one 5 times as well
	We - Nosotros	(Nohsohtrohs)	Pronounce this one 5 times
	You - Ustedes	(Oostedes)	This one 5 times as well
	They - Ellos	(Eyohs)	5 times with this as well
	It - Eso/ Esto	(Eso/Esto)	This one 5 times as well

Learning Step 4

The following are essential to any conversation:

Magic Words

Practice them!

Lesson 3: Part 1

Let us introduce a few words that are essential in any conversation

An/A	=	un uno / una unos / unas	Yes No	= Si = No
The	=	El La Los Las	At	= En el (lugar) En los (lugares) A las (horas)
And	=	Y	To	= A
With	=	Con	That	= Eso (señalar) Que (enfatizar)
Or	=	O	This	= Esto/Estos

Lesson 3: Part 2

What	=	Cuál, Qué	But	=	Pero
When	=	Cuándo	Whose	=	De quién
Where	=	Dónde	Who	=	Quién
Why/Because	=	Porqué	Which	=	Cuál
Whether	=	Bien sea, O	How	=	Cómo
To	=	A	For	=	Por, para
From	=	De, Desde	While	=	Mientras
How Many	=	Cuántos	Whom	=	Con quién
For	=	Para, por	As	=	Tal como
More than	=	Más que	How Much	=	Cuánto cuesta

A

A: Un, Uno, Una, Unos, Unas
About To: A punto De
Against: En Contra De
Although: Aunque, Aun Cuando
And: Y
As…As: Tan…Como
At (place): En La, En El, La(s)
At What Time: A Qué Hora
A Little: Poco, Poquito
Above: Arriba De
Ago: Hace
Already: Listo, Ya
And Now, What: Y Ahora Qué
As Long As: Mientras Que
At (hour): A las
Awful: Desagradable
A Little Bit: Un Poco
After: Después
All: Todo
Also: También
Another: Otro

As Soon As: Tan Pronto Como
At this Moment: En Este Momento
A Lot: Mucho
Afterwards: Luego, Después
All Day: Todo El Día
Always: Siempre
Anybody: Cualquiera
About: Acerca De
Again: De Nuevo
Almost: Casi
Amusing: Divertido
As: Tan, Tal Como
Appointed: Ser Nombrado
At This Time: En este Momento

B

Barely: Casi
Between: Entre, En El Medio De
Butter: Mantequilla
Because: Porque
Bit: Un Poco De

By: Por, De
Before, Antes
Both: Ambos
By The Way: A Propósito
Behind: Detrás De
Breakdown: Ruptura
Below: Debajo
But: Pero

C

Careful: Cuidado
Caution: Atencion, Cautela
Certain: Cierto (a)
Careful: Cuidado
Caution: Atencion, Cautela
Certain: Cierto (a)

D

Dear: Querido
Difficult: Difícil
Departure: Salida, Partida
Despite: A Pesar De

Detour: Desviación
Divided By: Dividido Por

F
Fair: Feria, Justo
Fine: Bueno
Further: Más Aún
Far: Lejos
For: Para
Fault: Culpa, Falla
For The Reason: Por La Razón
Feasible: Factible, Posible
Few: Poco
From: De

G
Generally: Generalmente
Good: Bueno (a)

H
Half: Medio, La Mitad

How Long: Cuánto Tiempo
Heavy: Pesado
How Much: Cuánto
How: Cómo
Hot: Caliente

I
If: Si
Impossible: Imposible
In front of: En Frente De
In good health: En Buena Salud
Inside: Dentro, Adentro
It is necessary: Es Necesario
Immediately: En Seguida, Inmediatamente, De Inmediato
Improbable: Improbable
In case of: En Caso De
In order that: En Orden De Que
Instead of: En Vez De
It could be: Pudiera Ser
In: En

In case that: En Caso Que
In order to: En Orden A
In spite of: Aun A Pesar De
It maybe: Puede ser
Important: importante
In a hurry: Apurado (a)
Included: Incluido
In the habit of: En El Hábito
Interesting: interesante

J
Just: Justo

K
Keep: Mantener
Kind: Amigable, Agradable, Clase, Tipo

L
Lacking: Carente de/ Desprovisto de
Latest: Lo último
Least: Menos

Lesson 3: Part 2

Likely: Probable
List: Lista
Low: Bajo
Large: Grande
Left: Izquierda
Little: Pequeño, Poco
Last: Ultimo, Ultima
Leftover: Sobrante, Lo que queda
Long: Largo
Late: Tarde
Looks Like: Parece tal como
Later: Mas Tarde
Less: Menos
Late: Tarde
Looks Like: Parece tal como
Later: Mas Tarde
Less: Menos

M
Made In: Hecho en
Mrs.: La Señora

M
Made In: Hecho en
Mrs.: La Señora
Many: Muchos
Much: Mucho
Maybe: Quizás
Merely: Apenas
Miss.: La Senorita
More: Más

N
Named (to be): Ser Llamado
Neither: Ninguno
Nothing: Nada
Narrow: Estrecho
Never: Nunca
Now: Ahora
Near: Cerca De
New: Nuevo
Nearby: Cerca
Next: Próximo
Necessary: Necesariamente

Next to: Al Lado De
Not: No

O
Obvious: Obvio
On: En, Sobre
Open: Abierto
Outside: Afuera
Odd: Extraño
On Call: De Guardia
Or: O
Over: Sobre
Of: De
Once: Una Vez
Other: Otro
Overcome: Superar
Of course: Por Supuesto
Ongoing: En Proceso
Otherwise: De Otra Manera
Overlook: Inspeccionar
Often: A Menudo

Only: Únicamente
Out: Afuera

P

Percent; Por ciento
Point: Punto
Push: Empujar
Perhaps: Quizás
Probable: Probable
Pleasant: Agradable
Problem: Problema
Perfectly: Perfecto
Program: Programa
Please: Por Favor
Pull: Tirar, Halar

Q

Question: Pregunta
Quite Enough: Suficiente, Bastante

R

Ready: Listo

Repeat: Repetir
Routine: Rutina
Regularly: Regularmente
Right Away: Pronto
Responsible: Responsable
Right Now: Ahora Mismo
Ridiculous: Ridículo
Relative: Pariente,
Relativamente

S

See you Later: Hasta
Luego
Sir: Señor
Something: Algo
Still: Todavía
Several: Varios
So: Tan, Entonces
Somewhat: Algo
Stop: Alto, Pare
Show Me: Muéstrame
Some: Algo, Algunos

So Much: Mucho
Subject: Tema, Sujeto
Side: Lado
Somebody: Alguien
Soon: Pronto
Sure: Seguro
Similar: Similar
Someone: Alguien
Specific: Específico
Somewhere: En Algún Lugar

T

Task: Tarea
The: El, La, Los, Las
Together: Juntos
Too (also): También
There Will Be: Habrá
That: Eso, Esa, Que
There: Allá
Through: A Través
Those: Aquellos (as)
Therefore: Por Consiguiente/
Por Lo Cual

Lesson 3: Part 2

There: Allá
These: Estos, Estas
To: A
Too Much: Demasiado
There is/are: Hay
Thick: Grueso
Tomorrow: Mañana
This Evening: Esta Noche
There Have Been: Han Estado
This: Esto, Esta
Thing: Cosa
Tonight: Esta Noche
There was/were: Hubo
There Would Be: Habría

U
Underneath: Debajo De
Unlikely: Difícil, Improbable
Unwilling: Sin Deseos
Under: Debajo
Up: Arriba
Until: Hasta
Useful: Útil

Understood: Entendido
Unless: A Menos Que
Unfortunately:
Desafortunadamente
Unpleasant: Desagradable

V
Very: Muy

W
Warm: Caliente
Why: Por qué
Where To: A dónde
Without: Sin
With: Con
Whatever: De Cualquier Manera
Whereby: A Través De Lo Cual
Whoever: Quien Quiera Que Sea
Watch Out: Cuidado
Wide: Ancho
Who: Quién
With Me: Conmigo
Whether: Bien Sea

Well: Bien
Which: Cual
With you: Contigo
Whole: Completo
Whereabouts: Donde Se
Encuentre, Paradero
Wet Paint: Pintura Fresca
What: Que, Cual
When: Cuando
Where: Donde
Whenever: Cuando Sea
Which: Cual
With you: Contigo
Within: Dentro De
While: Mientras
Who: Quien
Whole Completo
Without: Sin
Whose: De quien

Y
Yet: Todavia
Yield: Ceder El Paso

Learning Step 5

Reflexives and Possessives

are essential to complete a sentence

Practice them, emphasize the pronunciation

Lesson 3: Part 3

Reflexive / Reflexivo

Spanish/English/Spelling   Examples

Me (Meh) Me	Call me	**Llámame**
Le (Leh) You	Bring you	**Traerle**
Le (Leh) Him	Take him	**Llevarle**
La (Lah) Her	Invite her	**Invítarla**
Nos (Nohs) Us	Get us	**Búscanos**
Les (Lehs) You	Buy for you	**Cómprales**
Les (Lehs) Them	Write them	**Escríbeles**
Lo (Loh) It	Sell it	**Véndelos**

You	**have**	**to go**	**to take him**	**home**
Usted	tiene que	ir	a llevarle	a casa
Usted	le tiene que	ir	a llevar	a casa
He	**can**	**come**	**to see me**	**later**
El	puede	venir	a verme	luego
El	me puede	venir	a ver	luego
They	**want**	**to bring**	**her to see**	**you**
Ellos	la quieren	traer	a ver	le
They	**are**	**trying**	**to call**	**today**
Ellos	le están	tratando	de llamar	hoy

Possessive / Posesivo

Examples   Spanish/English/Spelling

My home	**Mi casa**	**Mi**	(Mee)	My
Your car	**Su coche**	**Su**	(Soo)	Your
His son	**Su hijo**	**Su**	(Soo)	His
Her pet	**Su mascota**	**Su**	(Soo)	Her
Our boat	**Nuestro barco**	**Nuestro** (Nooehstro)		Our
Your dad	**Vuestro padre**	**Vuestro** (Vooehstro)		Your
Their idea	**La idea de ellos**	**De ellos** (de-eyohs)		Their
Its tail	**Su cola**	**Su**	(Soo)	Its

You	**are**	**welcome to**	**our**	**house**
Usted	es	bienvenido a	nuestra	casa
She	**is**	**driving**	**my**	**car**
Ella	está	manejando	mi	coche
He	**has**	**to bring**	**my**	**son**
El	tiene que	traer	a mi	hijo
They	**want**	**to take**	**my**	**wife**
Ellos	quieren	llevar	a mi	esposa
Today	**I want**	**to go**	**to my**	**studio**
Hoy	yo quiero	ir	a mi	estudio

Notes on Reflexives : In Spanish a reflexive can also be placed right after the noun (at the very beginning of the phrase), it is preferable this way.

Examples :

I will bring them home
Yo voy a traerles a casa
Yo les voy a traer a casa

I want to take him to the airport
Yo quiero llevarle a el aeropuerto
Yo le quiero llevar al aeropuerto

I have to go to purchase the medicines for him
Yo tengo que ir a comprar le las medicinas
Yo le tengo que ir a comprar las medicinas

I can prepare de food for you at twelve
Yo puedo prepararles la comida a las doce
Yo les puedo preparar la comida a las doce

Learning Step 6

The Infinitive Verbs

Are the foundation of this course they are used almost identically both in English and Spanish

Practice them!

What is an Infinitive Verb?

1) Well, it starts with a "To" in English and ends with a "R" in Spanish

    Example: <u>to</u> call   <u>to</u> come   <u>to</u> go   <u>to</u> eat

               llamar   venir   <u>ir</u>   comer

2) It's never the 1st. verb (as it can't be conjugated)

    You can't say in English   I to call   I to come   I to go   I to eat

    You can't say in Spanish   Yo llamar   Yo venir   Yo ir   Yo comer

3) But it's always used after the 2nd. Infinitive Verb.

    Example: I   want   to go   to eat

             Yo quiero   ir   a comer

             She wants   to come   to visit

             Ella quiere   venir   a visitar

This course is built around the Infinitive Verbs

In English, infinitive verbs are used all the time:
I want to go to eat now.
He wants to come to visit you.

Hispanics use The Infinitive Verbs the same way

All the time and in the same way we do !

I	want	to go	to eat	now
Yo	quiero	ir	a comer	ahora
He	wants	to come	to visit	you
El	quiere	venir	a visitar	le

SMILE ☺ Both sentences mirror each other , except for the Spanish vowel de la vocal "a" (ah) which is added in front of the 2nd infinitive verb .

This course is built around <u>the Infinitive Verbs</u>

Here are more examples!

I	have	to take	you	She	wants	to watch TV	'til midnight
Yo	tengo que	llevar	le	Ella	quiere	mirar TV	hasta la medianoche
You	have	to bring	him	We	want	to go to shop	at noon
Usted	tiene que	traer	le	Nosotros	queremos	ir a comprar	al mediodía
He	has	to go to see	you	They	want	to give you	a surprise
El	tiene que	ir a ver	le	Ellos	quieren	dar le	una sorpresa
We	have	to try to get	there	You	want	to do him	a lot of good
Nosotros	tenemos que	tratar de llegar	allá	Usted	quiere	hacer le	mucho bien

The 8 Phrases mirror each other word by word except for the word "QUE" (Keh) which is added in Spanish to the verb "Tener" (To Have). "QUE" is used to denotes Duty or Responsibility after the verb "Tener" (To have). E.g., I have to go instead of Hold or Ownership (E.g. I have a family) and the letter "A" which is used by Hispanics ahead of the 2nd Verb and thereafter.

The two languages when spoken properly
Are spoken in the same way!

Lesson 4: Part 3

All You Need To Be Conversant in Spanish are "The Infinitive Verbs"
which are the Foundation of this method.

- The Infinitive Verbs are used the same way and even on the same spot in both Spanish and English .

- The Infinitive Verbs are never the 1st.Verb on a phrase :

> I   want   to have
> Yo quiero tener

- The Infinitive Verbs start with "To" in English: To have
And End with an R in Spanish :   Tener

- The Infinitive Verbs cannot be conjugated: I to have
                                                      Yo tener

- The Infinitive Verbs continue to be used on a phrase endlessly.
  In this sense the 2 languages are identical

> I   want to go to eat
> Yo quiero ir   a comer

- The 2nd. Infinitive Verb on a Spanish Phrase
  is always Preceded by an "A"

> I   want to go to sleep
> Yo quiero ir   a dormir

The infinitive Verbs enable through templates to be conversant in four tenses:
(1) Gerund-action, (2) Past Participle, (3) Future and (4) Conditional.